T0380820

"THE ANSWER !"

AuthorHouse™
1663 Liberty Drive
Bloomington, IN 47403
www.authorhouse.com
Phone: 1 (800) 839-8640

Because of the dynamic nature of the Internet, any web addresses or links contained in this book may have changed
since publication and may no longer be valid. The views expressed in this work are solely those of the author and do not
necessarily reflect the views of the publisher, and the publisher hereby disclaims any responsibility for them.

This book is printed on acid-free paper.

ISBN: 978-1-7283-2894-2 (sc)
ISBN: 978-1-7283-2903-1 (e)

Library of Congress Control Number: 2019915245

Print information available on the last page.

Published by AuthorHouse 09/30/2019

authorHOUSE

Contents

Virginia

you made my life complete

THE ANSWER !

Ed Rhymer

Also

by Ed Rhymer

The Reality of Love

The Blessed and The Damned

Live - Laugh - Love

&

Sincerely Smile Through it All

Virginia's Grace

HE

Setting The Stage

Many writers are very prolific in their endeavors. Some can spin a yarn almost daily and be well prepared for the periodic publications. There are also those who have the gift to express feelings and emotions in lofty prose. No criticism is offered for their abilities. Instead, they are appreciated and often very interesting reading.

Had it not been for a very few individuals, who encouraged and prodded my efforts, my writings would have never left my thoughts and dreams and reached the printed page.

Family is the primary focus in my life. There may be some who feel further revisiting the past serves no useful purpose. You would think there is very little left to say following five published works. Perhaps they are correct. Even so, history does need retelling, at least once. There should always be a record, as authentic as possible, for future generations to reference.

There may be those who will be disappointed in the content and nature of "The Answer !." No effort is made to soothe their concerns. Only direct and candid truths can hopefully gain their attention.

The contradictions and untruths existing in communications today can no longer be ignored. The misleading comments and outright lying by public officials is blatant and has become common practice in conversations. At times it is virtually impossible to gain an understanding of what is spoken.

That is often the politician's purpose. To influence the thinking and minds of the public and persuade them to follow their 'official line' of reason. Not the least of which, it serves politicians desires for power and control and therefore perpetuation of their position in office.

Recognition of the general tolerance and acceptance by the populace at large is the motivation of politicians.

People do not always think through a topic or event. Seldom do they stand as individuals or even as a group, with reasonably principled beliefs. Instead, they often choose to go along with the newness and excitement. Simply 'follow the crowd.'

Now this can be considered a contradiction within itself, as well as substantiation of many politicians motives and practices.

This knowledge is often taken to the extreme, with deliberate incitement of individuals and groups, who then take to the streets to disrupt reasonable and peaceful activities. These disruptions frequently result in rioting, looting and attacks upon law enforcement personnel.

The politicians simply stand back and take a lofty position, with outlandish charges, of the reasons for the disturbances and of the people who support legitimate causes.

It is my hope and prayer everyone who reads "The Answer !" will find some redeeming value. I trust their thinking will be influenced and they will choose to consider other thoughts and directions. Allow themselves to be challenged rather than taking the simple and perhaps the easy path through life.

I

The World The Way it Is

The majority of difficulties in our society can easily be traced to the multiplicity of laws and regulations. Many times they are passed and instituted on minuscule points with no reasonable issue involved. Primarily to satisfy the personal desire of the sponsor.

Playful outdoor activities are a lot of fun for children. This is not unknown. They are often indoors and outdoors, some temporary and others permanent in construction. Family participation in setting up an activity is exciting.

A family constructed an outdoor activity for their children. It provided a lot of fun and togetherness for the family. The activity was only intended to be temporary.

The public officials responded promptly upon learning of the effort and demanded the activity be removed or be subject to fines and penalties and even criminal charges were threatened.

This is not an uncommon occurrence or action by public officials. They often function on whims and personal interests rather than themselves be subject to reason or common sense.

Whatever happened to the simplicity of fun and happiness, especially within a family?

Power is a dangerous thing. Many politicians are addicted before they are elected in spite of their campaigning manifestations of wanting to 'serve the people.' Following their election they often become absolutely addicted. Very few, start out in their public life, truly serve and retire, with a record of complete honesty.

It is difficult to see how our country will be maintained as a democracy with so many radical propositions that have been presented in recent times.

Citizenship

Will someone please explain to me why a teen-aged youth should be granted the right to vote?

Generally, their level of education and maturity, comprehension and understanding of society's functional needs cannot be justified. Sure, there are those who are blessed with a higher level of maturity however, they are distinctly in the minority.

You often wonder what 'grading on the curve' actually means.

To be fair, the good and hardworking students should not suffer because of the few who are simply gifted at learning. Therefore, each student must have a fair chance at making the grade and achieving success. After all, the application of their individual skills and talents will serve an important function in the ongoing success of our democracy.

Many young people live in the moment, giving little thought to the sacrifices that made their 'today' possible.

This is not an indictment of young people. Nor is this an 'old fashioned' idea. You cannot make intelligent decisions based on whims, newness and the excitement generated by self-serving politicians, whose only purpose is often, to gain more voters they can influence.

There is no substitute for experience.

In addition, allowing convicted felons the right to vote is questionable at best. There may be a reasonable basis for denying them this right upon conviction, based upon their crime. However, to approach denial on a blanket retroactive basis is absurd. To reinstate every incarcerated individual's right to vote is equally ridiculous.

It should never be forgotten that their sociological shortcomings, mental and health difficulties often influence many individuals into criminal pursuits.

There should be reasonable debate on sensitive subjects such as this, without politicians influence or interference. That is truly the challenge.

Being American - Immigrants

Humanitarian assistance should always be afforded to immigrants regardless of their personal situation or where they came from. Many times the individuals simply cannot help themselves and it is every human's duty to offer aide and assistance wherever possible.

This is not a subject that merits debate. Either you are a citizen or you are not. Allowing immigrants to flow freely into the country without guidelines and management is absolutely beyond reason.

You must proceed through the appropriate process, to become a citizen, before you are eligible for the benefits available. Each and every immigrant, without exception. Immigrants simply cannot be allowed freedom of entry into our society without restrictions. They should not be allowed access to our society's benefits until they have earned that privilege.

Allowing uncontrolled access to the United States of America has reached a crisis stage. Efforts are being made to resolve this issue without any evident success. Constant conflicts and contradictions among politicians and political parties prevents any reasonable efforts at an orderly and legitimate process.

The current situation at our borders is a clear example. Consequently, requiring those immigrants already scattered throughout our society, to respond and be accountable, has become futile.

The problems regarding illegal immigrants are a direct responsibility of self-serving politicians. They have allowed these difficulties to manifest themselves for decades. Primarily to gain their support and that of radical, often anti-American groups.

Many immigrant individuals and families are well established in our society, hard working and making very notable contributions. Many of the young who were brought here, have been educated, advanced themselves and are now making their own contributions to society.

There should be no desire to conduct a mass roundup and deportation of these well established, law abiding individuals and families.

However, procedures should be clearly set forth and enforced to provide the opportunity for them to remain and enter the process to become citizens.

This issue alone could very well lead to the destruction of our society, as it was intended. The irresponsible and criminal elements among unaccounted for immigrants has led to increased crime. The burdens upon our society as a result are enormous. The drain on resources, demands on society and resulting financial requirements are virtually out of control.

Law and order is a basic element of a peaceful society. There must be rules and regulations to assist each citizen's utilization of the benefits afforded. Likewise, those individuals, who are not entitled, should not be allowed access.

Respect for law and order has reached a point where the dissenters are afforded the privilege of deciding what they will obey. A 'do as you please' attitude has become so prevalent, far too many people seem to feel this is the appropriate and correct way of life. It is not uncommon to display thoughts and attitudes and actions that are independent of any respect for others.

Of course, politicians take advantage of these problems to demand more use of resources, increased taxes and more unearned benefits to immigrants.

It has become virtually impossible to review the bulk of the United States Code.

The majority of problems in our society are the result of compounding laws and regulations. As mentioned, they are often instituted over minuscule points, without any reasonable basis or issue being involved.

The code should be re-instituted to the original intent. The absolutely unnecessary restrictions and regulations placed upon citizens should be removed.

Of course, the related expenses upon the citizens reduce their freedom and ability to influence proper legislation.

These difficulties feed directly into the narrative of many politicians. Especially those who are inclined to favor a socialist or communist society with extensive government controls.

Then, where is freedom and democracy? They are simply incompatible with a socialistic or communistic society and governmental controls.

II
Principles - Beliefs

"Exalt the Lord our God, and worship at his holy hill; for the Lord our God is holy." Psalm 99 - vs 9 - kjv

This may be considered by some as being 'out of context' with the overall subject and purpose of this commentary. However, the challenge is to stop and think.

Every single thought deserves to be assessed and evaluated in relation to the subject. Never allow yourself to be caught up in the tension and pressure of the moment.

Words have a clear and defined meaning and they should not be distorted or interpreted. Nor should they be couched in excessive verbiage which is often used to serve an unprincipled purpose.

There is no compromise in right or wrong. Only when perhaps, 'maybe' or 'I don't know' are involved.

The demand for respect should always be justified by duty, responsibility and honor.

Communications

The population has virtually exploded in the past century and has experienced a steadily increasing rise since the 1960's. With the difficulties and conflicts resulting from the added freedom and uncontrolled influx of illegal immigrants, it is safe to say, the situation is out of control.

Development is so rapid that changes are occurring too often for understanding and adequate assimilation into society. There is simply no opportunity in many cases for proper training and adjustment. Outside influences have become such a force they are dominate in many situations.

Decisions among individuals and generally throughout our society are no longer based on the simplicity of right or wrong. Now, almost all decisions are rationalized, often without consideration for possibly unfavorable results.

This is without question, clearly reflected in the current discourse over abortion, racial relations, social welfare, medical care, and numerous other subjects.

It bears repeating that politicians are apparently unconcerned about maintaining consistency in providing for the welfare and needs of the populace. It is very clear their first priority is promoting themselves when their focus should be on the citizens. Especially the young, who are so susceptible to unfavorable influences.

Abortion

Here again, would someone please explain to me why abortion should be such a free-will and rampant choice in our society?

Whatever happened to parents teaching their children the proper morals and principles regarding human relationships, especially those that may involve sexual activity?

Whatever happened to the dignity and respect for human life?

Now you can easily debate these are different times. Some things should always remain basic to human existence and relationship with others. It may be considered overly simplistic however, there should be no debate over right or wrong.

The public discourse regarding when conception occurs and when does the viability of a fetus begin are astounding.

Look closely! The politicians are ridiculously making judgments, issuing executive orders, pushing for legislation and marshaling groups of people in favor of their proposals.

This is absolute insanity. Since when do they feel they have become so powerful they can stand in the place of God?

School administrators have allowed themselves to become more sensitive to what the public may think rather than the welfare of the students. It seems education is no longer their primary concern.

It is clear in news reports, day after day, true or untrue, fingers are being pointed to the student rather than teachers or administrators. Student's allegations are not always reported.

One incident related administrators and a counselor did not report a student's allegation she had been assaulted by a teacher. The teen was instructed to apologize and hug the teacher, then she was suspended. An indictment was also handed down in the matter.

I do not believe I can be convinced this is the appropriate way to handle matters of this nature. Of course, to ignore students complaints is wrong in any circumstance. This would not seem to be a very mature or intelligent way to handle the matter, whether or not the complaint is true or untrue.

It seems to me the current generation and perhaps more have been led down the path of ignoring morals and propriety, by individuals and groups who desire to perpetuate their philosophy of a freewill society without restraints or restrictions. This has been referred to in the past as, 'don't rock the boat.'

It very well may be the boat has already capsized.

Think of the young people, boys and girls, who have taken so called 'body art' to extremes, with tattoos placed all over their body to the point of being offensive to the eyes and often becoming unrecognizable.

Highlight this with slouchy, unkept clothing and multiple rings, bracelets and necklaces and body piercings in every conspicuous location. And often some that are not. Even facial hair has been taken to extremes and hair length is not always maintained in a clean or reasonably respectable manner.

These practices are continued by many well into adulthood and as a senior citizen.

In many cases they wonder why it is difficult to be acceptable in some public facilities and find gainful employment or acceptance on some levels of society.

Where is pride and self-respect?

I am sure those who study these individuals, for a degree of understanding, have had considerable difficulty arriving at justifiable reasons for these practices.

Virtually everything begins with parental training and education. It is apparent many individuals 'came up short' in those phases of life.

Meanwhile the homeless and derelict population continues to grow and social welfare programs are rapidly becoming unable to meet the demands. Of course, the politicians have allowed these problems to become a crisis. The solutions are very apparent. They are simply ignored.

Social Welfare

Welfare programs have been expanded to such an extent that more and more people are seeking the benefits. Many programs are available without cost to the individual or family. Oftentimes, they are provided without having been earned or even being entitled in any manner.

So many programs have come forward there is often insufficient funding and support. This excess availability inevitably leads to reliance and dependence. It would be nearly impossible to explain each one.

Certainly there is justification for taking care of the less fortunate in our society.

There are numerous reasons why some have not had opportunities for a relatively consistent life. Among them are training, education, employment availability, health conditions and many others. These individuals should not be neglected.

Medicare is a basic benefit afforded in our society. However, it should not be expanded to provide care from conception to the end of life. To do so, relieves individuals from the responsibility for the life they chose to create. Nor should it relieve them of their responsibility to society.

A basic health benefit is vaccines. They are provided and enhanced to treat many common illnesses and for disease prevention. This is a government program and available to everyone, without charge. Not to take advantage of this benefit risks serious illness, even disability or death, to the children and of course, exposure and spreading of the disease to others.

Yet, due to whatever reason, many parents refuse to have their children vaccinated.

Many objections to this and other programs are emanating from immigrants. Of course, most are relatively new to the United States and the importance of these programs is not known or perhaps even available in their home countries.

It is also noted objections are often for personal reasons however, many are religious in nature. The religious beliefs of an individual or group should not be condemned. However, their beliefs should not be forced upon others, instead the primary interest should be the health and welfare of society.

Evidently many did not take heed from their parents or grandparents experiences over the previous years.

LGBTQ

This subject has been pushed to the forefront of our society. Laws are being changed almost daily, consequently disrupting basic functions in society, without regard for the results. Now that the individuaLs involved have gained a more conspicuous voice they are simply continuing forward on the basis of whatever they wish should be granted.

True, no one should tell another what their choices should be in life. Whether or not you may personally approve is not the issue. Every citizen is entitled to the benefits of our society.

Likewise, individuals who choose this lifestyle have no right to force acceptance upon the remainder of society. Especially, with overly conspicuous pronouncements and demands. They should live according to the laws and regulations which govern all other citizens conduct. They do not deserve any more consideration or privileges than are afforded to everyone else.

Marijuana

Can you believe it? The United States has become overrun with illegal narcotics and yes, marijuana is a narcotic. There is no question as to its origins. Money, power and influence have lifted it to the level of acceptance.

Illegal drugs is a major industry throughout the world. Enormous amounts of money are involved. Every means possible is being used to bring them into our country for distribution and sale. This further complicates the efforts to control illegal immigration and the movement of people and cargo in and out of our ports of entry.

Politicians are not assisting. Instead they are providing the 'slippery slope' to further facilitate the downward spiral.

Laws are passed as to the amount of a narcotic in possession before it is considered a crime and subject to prosecution. Sentences are also issued in the same fashion.

Marijuana has now reached the stage of legalization in many states.

Cannabis, hemp, marijuana, cbd oil, by any other name are all the same. Everyone is attempting to get on the money side of this subject *in distribution and sales. Retail shops are now open, individually and as chains.*

Colorado and California have long led the way. People have been drifting to these states and others, for decades, due to the readily available narcotics and unfettered access to welfare programs.

The attitudes and resulting problems that contributed to this explosion have spread throughout the United States.

The only reason promoted for the legalization of marijuana is its' so-called medical benefits. This justification is absolutely asinine. Marijuana is simply another narcotic used for a 'high.' There are dozens of medications that are available by prescription. And they, more than adequately, treat any legitimate medical issue or addictive desire.

Producers and supporters are simply attempting to side-step FDA requirements. They are defying the government, actually daring, with mass production and distribution.

It can be easily foreseen this could eventually be considered a disease, like alcohol and therefore subject to medical care and government benefits.

With the experiences over tobacco, alcohol and now narcotics becoming an accepted part of society it is easy to wonder what will be the next change.

Will the next step be to negotiate with the 'drug lords,' south of the border, over import quotas and distribution rights?

The stupidity of it all.

The government is losing control. Crimes have skyrocketed. Jails and prisons are so overrun they have become a revolving door. Criminals are being released back onto the streets to make room for the influx.

Homeless are so abundant they are causing traffic problems and a drain on resources. Tent cities have sprung up across the country. Now they are occupying public facilities and buildings, without constraints.

Hospitals and medical facilities have become so overcrowded their personnel are having considerable difficulty dealing with the related health and narcotic addicted issues. This results in a considerable burden on society for expanded resources and increased medical expenses for the remaining citizens.

The politicians are turning a blind eye to the increasing problems and the potential for complete loss of control.

Sanctuary cities and the victim support philosophy are contributing to the lack of law enforcement.

Many states are consistently pursuing for federal grants to assist with these problems.

'Grants:' The grand opening for governmental control.

There seems to be no end.

Stop! Look! Listen!

How quick we forget the past. The lessons of history are sometimes difficult to learn and accept. And especially remember, when they are methodically removed from the classroom.

Does anyone recall the era of prohibition?

An era when moral and principled people opposed gambling and drinking, forcing politicians to respond by passing laws to prevent these practices.

Speakeasies developed and the modern day version of rum-running. Alcohol was brought into the country by the criminal elements. Gambling and drinking went underground and continued to thrive.

These actions were only a temporary setback for politicians. The loss of government revenue quickly became apparent. A few short years later the politicians passed new laws and the situation was completely reversed.

Alcohol is very big business. Many state governments have their own retail sales stores. Gambling never seems to cease. Casinos are expanding into many states and lotteries instituted as well.

Tobacco has long been a source for opposition and support with related health issues that are a drain on society. Only gradual changes have occurred. Instead the difficulties compounded.

Now there is, 'Juul,' 'Vaping,' current forms of 'Hookah.' Some cultural practices introduced by immigrants are not always beneficial to society.

Entrepreneurs and criminals will always find a way.

The cycle continues.

Aspersions and blame and responsibility are cast toward any individual or group that criticizes or opposes the politicians efforts to extend programs rather than institute positive changes.

When or where will it all end?

More taxes and rules and regulations are instituted. Prices are increased and more restrictions to discourage higher wages. Meanwhile the general populace becomes more oppressed and the politicians perpetuate their position.

Not to be forgotten are the frustrations of the people. They have arrived at this stage of our society, with population expansion and the mass of illegal immigrants contributing to these frustrations.

The number of law enforcement personnel are insufficient in comparison to the population growth. They are simply unable to deal with the complaints, let alone control individual situations. As a result these frustrations frequently erupt in violence. Shootings are occurring daily, with people being killed and many others injured.

Race

Is this truly a legitimate issue?

Perhaps the commentary on LGBTQ should follow the discourse on Race. They are often incorporated simultaneously in conversation. This is misleading for they are two distinctly different subjects.

The free-will vitriol bandied about in the news media and among the populace has become unintelligible at times.

Only the rainbow colored heat waves can be seen emanating from the words used to express criticism and hatred. Racist, homophobe, bigot, xenophobe, chauvinist, supremacist and on and on.

Derogatory words roll off their tongues with regularity and are used each time they become frustrated the dialogue does not follow their 'line of reasoning.'

It is very evident today, the news media makes every effort to shape the news. They no longer simply report the information and facts and allow the people to draw their own conclusions.

Whatever happened to intelligent even tempered conversation?

Racist, a word directed at any individual or group, regardless of the reason, especially those who are in opposition to people of color and to any of their proposals or decisions.

Use of the word racist has become so prevalent it is now utilized for virtually all forms of discrimination. As everyone should know, the word discrimination has a definition and application very separate from the negative aspects, applied today, of race.

Let us be fair. Racist and racism are descriptive words being carried over from the era of slavery in the United States.

Slavery was evident in many countries around the world and was brought to America, with the initial settlers, centuries ago.

When the settlers began to develop their society and governance it became apparent the practice of slavery required consideration as an issue.

The founding documents of America clearly establish the intent. They should not be interpreted to suit an individual or an era. Freedom was a primary word.

Our society has survived by devotion to the founding principles. Discarding these principles is self-destructive.

Progress has been made. Practices have become normalized. Equality has been well established.

It is often overlooked that 'people of color' does not singularly apply only to African Americans. The United States of America is a culturally diverse nation of many nationalities and cultures. One group should not and cannot attempt to claim exclusivity.

There are those who do not accept change or improvements. Self-serving individuals, who feel they are and should continue to be, entitled to whatever they wish. They have an attitude of being perpetually offended and turn a blind eye to progress.

Activists and politicians, encourage and continue to perpetuate this attitude in our society.

Entrepreneurs have contributed considerably to the ongoing racial emphasis. Many radio and television networks, magazines and other media are exclusively culturally oriented. These endeavors are established businesses and monetarily based, of course. Nevertheless, they often perpetuate the emphasis and contribute to the cultural divide in America.

Individual and group cultural heritages should not be ignored. Even so, the point has been reached where we may no longer be able to successfully move away from the distinction of racial differences.

There must be a way to remove the attachment of the subject of race from politics, in order that politicians may be unable to utilize it to incite the populace in a negative and hateful manner and thereby perpetuate their position of power.

It should always be remembered that activists and politicians are continuing to perpetuate this disruption. They could make an about face at any time.

Our savior is needed, more than ever.

The stability of society and the equality of the citizens is essential for progress. When it is sacrificed for the sake of a singular group everyone will suffer. The danger is that society may very well break apart.

The simple solution to racism is to accept and assimilate into society. Become part of society, receive the full benefits and discard dissension from your mind.

The general populace only sees an issue when deliberate actions are taken to foment discord.

Democracy cannot survive without the rule of law and order.

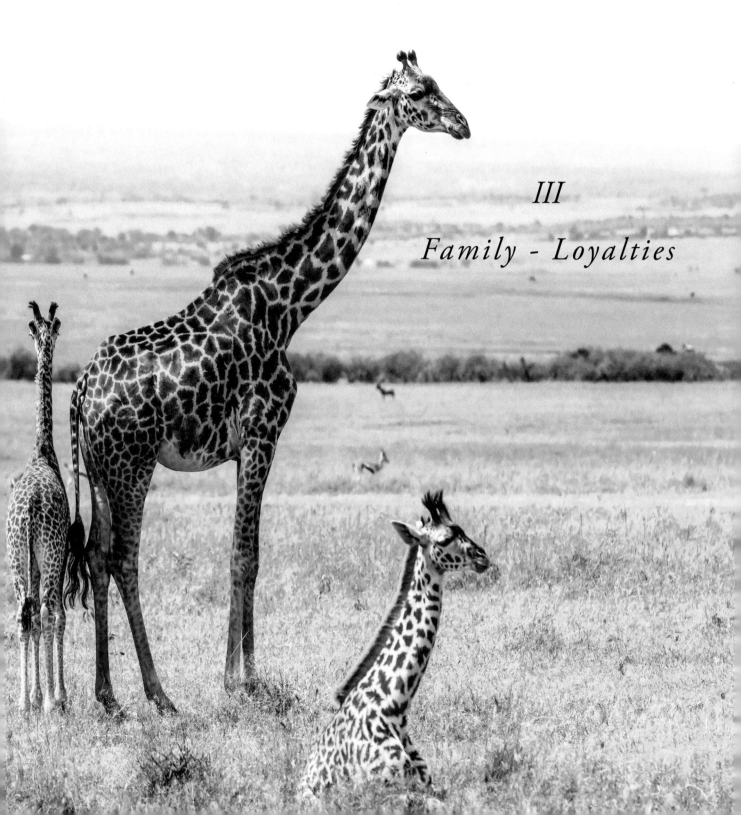

III

Family - Loyalties

A truth learned many years ago is assumption and presumption do not go hand-in-hand, with perception and understanding.

Family! The most important concept in humanity. From the very first family to today, family remains the essential pathway to a consistent and successful life.

Each one of us is born into a family. We do not have a choice in the matter. Our parents, who made that choice, have a monumental responsibility and duty to ensure our welfare and safety is provided, to the very best of their ability.

Loyalties! The first duty of parents is to the children they chose to bring into this world. The health and welfare of the children, training and education and assistance stepping into life on their own will always remain parents fundamental duty. Self-interest is secondary to that responsibility.

It is not always possible for every parent to fulfill that charge. The demands are great and the challenges often formidable.

What is the solution when those responsibilities and duties become difficult or cannot be fulfilled?

Many times assistance is sought from other family members or friends. Oftentimes the responses are insufficient. In those instances we turn to the community.

For many it is difficult to expose your family difficulties to public scrutiny. However, the important thing is to forget yourself and maintain your responsibility and duty to your family.

The social welfare programs are numerous and available for almost all aspects of human needs. Especially those involving health, food, clothing and shelter. Many of these programs have the availability of transportation to facilitate your access or in bringing the aid to your home.

Not to be forgotten is public education, which is available to every citizen. There is much to be accomplished in this area. Uniformity in teaching standards and classroom conditions. Especially equality in wages across the country.

Unions have made major contributions to society. Especially in business, industry and education. However, they have also been guilty of multiple and complicated problems. Their push and demands for influence and control in an individual area can be considered the primary cause of the imbalance in operational costs and wages.

These programs were created, as the need arose in a generation. They have been improved upon and the truly beneficial programs have become a permanent part of our society.

The challenge for our society and government has been to ensure each program is properly supported and waste avoided and the benefits are readily available for each citizen.

As discussed earlier, societal and governmental programs are not always carried out or maintained as initially intended. Non-citizens often become included in the programs.

When difficulties or demands in administration arise they are often met with expansion and compounding of the benefits rather than complying with the initial intent or seeking more efficient means. This often results in a citizen's loss of opportunity and benefits.

As mentioned the United States of America has always been humane and generous to its' citizens and this thoughtfulness and generosity has often been extended to the rest of the world. This is our hallmark and a primary basis for the continuous immigration to our shores.

IV
Faith - A Higher Calling

When you start each day with a question you often wonder how or whether an answer will be provided. More importantly, if so, who will provide the answer.

Should you be a person of faith then you know who will provide an answer. How is not important. When becomes meaningless.

Trust and reliance are the foundation stones of faith. You simply know that the answer will be more than satisfactory. It will provide all the answers necessary because it will come from the Lord God.

Once this level of confidence and strength of faith, in an individual life is reached, there is never any doubt.

And so it is! This is an entirely different world we live in today. This was very apparent well prior to September 11 th. The individuals who feel surprised were simply isolated within themselves. That in itself is not surprising, for a great many people live a life centered around themselves.

It is sad to see so many people thinking of their own self-gratification; to feel they are in charge of their own existence. As a consequence, they become excited and fearful whenever an event touches or threatens their personal situation. At those times, to learn they really have no control is truly frightening.

God grants us time and a place in life, for a purpose. Many try to reach beyond the simplicity of that truth. It is so clear and easily understood. After all, it is intended that even children can comprehend. Faith and trust in Him.

Everyone is different. It is very difficult to tell the depth of a person's beliefs or faith. Certainly not from simply looking at them or meeting them or even spending time with them. Acceptance is a basic element of faith.

Believing that God will protect and provide is the strength of faith.

Accepting that He has control allows His comforting assurance to develop within our hearts and minds. Then, when the shadows of night pass our way, we know that our soul will be safe.

After Thoughts

The world in which we find ourselves today is very much like a jungle.

Governmental controls in many phases of daily life have reached the point where they restrict an individual's ability to be creative and often productive.

Guidelines and regulations are necessary for order and effectiveness in society. However they are often utilized to control thinking and productive processes and channel activities to the self-interest of politicians. Service to the people is then forgotten.

The demand has become great for the ingenuity, talents and skills necessary to navigate this jungle of rules and regulations. Finding and encouraging individuals into those pursuits is the new challenge.

Reading the news daily can be very distressing. Watching distorted, opinionated television shows even more so.

Why is it necessary to be so negative and critical of almost everything and everyone and yes, even lie and deny to achieve your idea of right?

Times do change. What is liked, enjoyed today is very different from half a century ago. For that matter, even 10 or 15 years ago. The world is moving entirely too rapidly. Why is this so? It is completely unnecessary. Fast living was once referred to as 'burning the candle at both ends.' That has no allowance for living.

Today it seems the pressures of society are forcing individuals to fall in step with the rapid pace. Conversations and commentaries have become so rapid it is difficult to understand what is spoken.

Individuals have lost the appreciation of living life. Little value is placed upon today. Why is this so? Don't people realize that life is a series? Didn't their parents teach them that life must be enhanced each day, with the foresight of always seeking tomorrow?

Gone are letters and postcards and often telephone calls to family and friends.

Today it is the I-phone, I-pad and other devices.

There is also the use of social media. An area where an individual's intelligence is expressed in a limited number of characters and personal information exposed to the world. Social media has become a means for malcontents to express themselves in a hurtful and hate filled manner.

Improvements are essential to a progressive society. However, all changes do not fully reflect a positive approach.

The development of electronic devices and the extensive utilization of these forms of communication has caused significant damage to human relationships. Expansion of areas of learning and comprehension are no longer emphasized in the oversimplified world of electronic communications.

Physical education and activity participation was once a regular part of school curriculums. Their emphasis has been reduced and even eliminated in many educational systems.

Activities should be encouraged that involve physical participation among youths, especially outdoors. Parents and other adults should become involved in teaching and participating in these activities.

Whatever became of Boys and Girls Clubs and Community Centers? Neighborhood playgrounds and swimming pools?

Broadening of horizons is not an area of emphasis in today's society. The human element may have lost its' meaning.

How can you develop and function in relation to other people when you no longer fraternize and socialize face to face?

Character must be evaluated to facilitate discussion and interaction. A person or subject simply cannot be assessed in a limited electronic exchange.

Suggested Solutions

Our borders should be closed and entry allowed only for those who qualify for asylum and are prepared to follow our lawful rules and procedures. Methods must be established to follow those individuals until they complete qualifications for citizenship.

Employment opportunities should be made available to citizens prior to being filled by those who cross our borders for work. Businesses who ignore rules and regulations in order to employ migrants for the cheap labor should be penalized.

Visa requirements should be enforced. Many people remain in the United States long after their visa expires. They become part of the unaccountable group, including illegal immigrants, which expands the related difficulties and problems in our society.

Campaign finance reform should be foremost with limitations on donations and expenditures by the candidates. Candidates should then be more equal and can campaign primarily on their leadership abilities, experience and proposals.

Term limits should be established for politicians, with requirements for them to deal with the issues and work to resolve the problems, proposed in their campaigns to qualify for reelection. They should promote their programs rather than themselves.

Citizens should be encouraged to become involved in the process and submit proposals to their congressional representative. The proposals should be properly submitted to Congress for research, investigation and debate prior to consideration for passage.

Each citizen should give back to their community and advocate for a positive and beneficial cause. They should devote time to serving and participating in programs that assist the needy and unfortunate in our society.

Citizens should also be encouraged to run for public office, especially those with experience in business and public service. Although many politicians are from the field of law, they do not have an exclusive right to run for office. They certainly do not have all the answers as to what best serves society.

Discontinue elected officials unlimited access to and use of government resources and funds. Their incomes and retirement benefits should be established consistent with the civil service system.

Lobbyists should be banned from freewill access to politicians and their offices as well as governmental departments. They should follow and participate in the process with all citizens.

Business and industry, financiers and entrepreneurs should compete, in the market place, on the basic principles of quality, price and service. Existing rules and regulations should be strengthened and enforced.

Anti-trust laws should also be strengthened with guidelines established and clearly defined to prevent monopolies. No single individual, company or corporation should be allowed to dominate their respective market.

This approach alone will contribute considerably to maintaining a stable economy and provide gainful employment for the majority of our citizens.

Programs should be emphasized that clearly assist new parents to develop their skills at caring for their child, training and preparing them for the challenges of growing up, maturing and becoming part of society.

Many charitable and presently existing programs could be easily discontinued or consolidated into this effort. After all, there is a great deal of duplicity in existing programs.

Access to welfare programs should not be allowed without some form of public service, or contribution to society, in return. This approach alone will significantly encourage individuals to help themselves. It will serve to lift them out of the homeless and derelict groups and show them the possibilities available.

Even more so, it will involve more and more individuals in serving, to improve our society as a whole.

Addicts should be required to submit to detoxification programs to qualify for governmental assistance in reestablishing their life.

Government influences and controls in citizens lives are seldom popular. However, a way must be found to encourage acceptance of limited regulations and controls in areas that are so damaging to the lives of our citizens.

The FDA has been prominent in regulation and control of products. Their duty and responsibility should be strengthened to prevent introduction of unhealthy products into the marketplace, until thorough research and tests are complete.

The freedom and open market approach in America has been used as justification for individuals and companies to initiate areas of enterprise.

This has been very evident in today's society with the actual ignoring of laws and regulations. Marijuana and Vaping are two glaring examples. Business efforts are initiated without following procedures for approval, licensing and legal establishment. Even to the point of flaunting their efforts and challenging the officials to take action against their efforts.

As mentioned earlier, law enforcement is simply unable to keep up with the explosion of the population. Even so, these unlawful businesses should be required to comply with the existing laws and regulations or be subject to closing of the establishment. Severe fines and penalties against the officers should also be considered.

Stricter requirements for an organization to qualify as a charity or foundation and therefore qualify for tax or other benefits. There should be very stringent controls of contributions and expenditure of funds.

Many of these suggested solutions would require difficult choices and sacrifice. Given thought, I am sure many additional, worthy suggestions could be brought forth for consideration.

Significant Laws and regulations have been instituted that allowed many of the problems to develop in our society. Far too many have allowed for duplication and compounding of issues. This truth must be accepted and the dedication of our citizens required to confront and seek resolutions, without delay.

About The Author

Family is and should be the primary focus in life, with everyone. Some may feel revisiting the past serves no useful purpose. You would think there is little that remains to say, following five published works. Perhaps they are correct. However, history does need retelling, at least once. There should be an authentic record for future generations to reference.